I0800648

STUDY GUIDE

Willing to Believe

R.C. Sproul

LIGONIER MINISTRIES
Renew your Mind.
LIGONIER.ORG | 800-435-4343

421 Ligonier Court, Sanford, FL 32771
E-mail: info@ligonier.org

Printed in China.

1

The Truth Shall Make You Free

MESSAGE INTRODUCTION

The nature of free will has been at the center of numerous controversies and debates throughout the history of the church. Two issues are central in the debate. The first is the relationship between free will and the sovereignty of God. The second has to do with the effects of the Fall upon man's will. In this lesson, Dr. Sproul introduces the topic of free will and discusses both of these questions.

LEARNING OBJECTIVES

1. To be able to explain what Jesus means when He tells the Pharisees that they are "slaves of sin."
2. To understand the basic difference between humanistic notions of free will and the Christian doctrine of free will.
3. To be able to define the two main theological questions involved in the question of free will.

QUOTATIONS

God hath endued the will of man with that natural liberty, that it is neither forced, nor by any absolute necessity of nature determined, to good or evil.

—The Westminster Confession of Faith, Ch. IX:1

A man is always free in every responsible volition, as much when he chooses, in violation of the law of God and conscience, as in conformity to it.

—A.A. Hodge

LECTURE OUTLINE

I. Introduction

   A. In John 8, Jesus becomes involved in a controversy with the Pharisees over the issue of freedom.
   B. In verse 32, Jesus makes the seemingly innocuous statement "'the truth shall make you free.'"
   C. The Jews object to the idea that they can be made free because it implies that they are in some kind of captivity.
   D. Jesus tells them that they are slaves of sin who need to be set free.
   E. If there is anything Jesus taught that is widely rejected today, it is the idea that we are by nature slaves of sin.

II. The controversy

   A. The Jews who disagreed with Jesus stood within the Old Testament tradition and knew about the Fall, but their belief system included a pagan understanding of humanity.
   B. They had an exalted view of the inherent goodness of human nature.
   C. The dominant view has continued to be the humanistic doctrine, which teaches that no matter how frequently we may stumble, evil is external to our hearts.
   D. Incredibly, two-thirds of evangelicals polled recently also said that man is basically good.
   E. Christians often blame problems on secular humanism, but Christians have undermined their own cause by embracing a humanist anthropology.
   F. This is largely due to our common notions of free will, ideas that do not come from Scripture but from pagan and humanistic sources.

III. The issue of free will

   A. Fundamentally, the question of free will relates to two distinct theological questions:
      i. What is the relationship between free will and the sovereignty of God?
      ii. How did the Fall and original sin affect man's free will?
   B. The question of the relationship between man's free will and God's sovereignty raises questions about determinism—the view that human decisions are determined by an external cause.
      i. One type of determinism is fatalism. According to fatalism, the destiny of individuals is grimly determined by entities such as the stars.
      ii. A second type of determinism is naturalistic determinism. According to this position, our decisions are caused by fixed natural causes such as biochemical reactions or external cultural conditioning.
   C. The question of the relationship between the Fall and man's free will essentially has to do with the extent to which the Fall has influenced our free will.

STUDY QUESTIONS

1. How did the Pharisees respond to Jesus' statement "'the truth shall make you free'"?
   a. They said, "You have a demon."
   b. They said, "What must we do to be saved?"
   c. They said, "We have never been in bondage to anyone."
   d. They tried to stone him.

2. What point was Jesus emphasizing in this dispute with the Pharisees?
   a. We are slaves of sin
   b. Truth is relative
   c. Slavery is a sin
   d. Truth is unknowable

3. What Old Testament doctrine should have prepared the Jews for Jesus' statement?
   a. Creation
   b. The Exile
   c. The Fall
   d. The Suffering Servant

4. What has been the dominant view of human nature in history?
   a. No matter how frequently man may stumble, evil is external to his heart.
   b. Fallen man is a slave of sin.
   c. Fallen man has damaged the image of God in which he was created.
   d. Man is as evil as he possibly can be.

5. What percentage of evangelicals polled claimed to believe that man is basically good?
   a. A very small percentage
   b. Two-thirds
   c. Almost 100 percent
   d. One-third

6. What teaching asserts that human decisions are determined by an external cause?
   a. Neo-orthodoxy
   b. Christianity
   c. Arminianism
   d. Determinism

7. According to ______________, the destiny of individuals is grimly determined by entities such as the stars.
    a. Fatalism
    b. Calvinism
    c. Naturalistic determinism
    d. Pelagianism

8. What is the name of the influential twentieth-century determinist that Dr. Sproul mentioned?
    a. Sigmund Freud
    b. B.F. Skinner
    c. Karl Barth
    d. C.S. Lewis

BIBLE STUDY

1. Read John 8:31–38. What does Jesus say about the relationship between sin and slavery? According to Jesus, what will make a slave free?

2. In John 14:6, what does Jesus declare Himself to be? How does this relate to John 8:31–38?

3. In John 8:33 and 39, the Jews to whom Jesus is speaking place much of their hope in their ancestry. They appeal to their blood relationship to Abraham. How does Jesus respond to this appeal?

4. Read Galatians 3:16. According to Paul, who is the Seed to whom the promises were made? Now read Galatians 3:29. Who else does Paul consider to be Abraham's seed? Upon what is inheritance of the Abrahamic promises now based, according to Paul—ability to trace one's lineage to Abraham or union with Christ?

5. How does Paul reinforce this understanding of the relationship of Jews to the Abrahamic promises in Romans 2:28–29?

6. Read Ephesians 2:11–13. Paul says in these verses that he is addressing Gentiles who have believed in Christ. Paul lists five things that were true of these Gentiles but no longer are true now that they have believed. What are the five things that Paul says characterized the Gentiles' state as unbelievers? Since, according to Paul, the opposites of those five things are now true of the Gentiles, list the five things that are now true of the Gentile believers.

DISCUSSION QUESTIONS

1. Why is it important to understand that the "truth" to which Jesus refers in John 8 is not merely an abstract conceptual truth?
2. Granting that the Jews to whom Jesus spoke missed His point, why is their claim that they never have been enslaved to anyone ironic? Discuss some ways in which modern Christians could fall into a similar type of self-deception.
3. Modern dispensationalism teaches that the Abrahamic promises still belong exclusively to the physical descendants of Abraham. Is such a doctrine defensible in light of the New Testament teaching in passages such as Galatians 3 and Ephesians 2?
4. Does infant baptism necessarily lead Christians to the same kind of false trust in their physical lineage that the Jews of Jesus' day expressed? Defend your answer.

APPLICATION

1. Meditate on Jesus' words in John 8. Consider what it means for you to have been a slave of sin. Consider what it means for God to have adopted you as a son.
2. If you were polled today, would you say that man is basically good? Why is it important for your Christian life to understand that fallen man is not inherently good?
3. Do you ever find yourself lapsing into a pessimistic fatalism? What can you do to avoid that non-Christian attitude?
4. In your prayers, remember to thank God for setting you free, for adopting you as His child, and for giving you a lasting hope.

FOR FURTHER STUDY

Sproul, R.C. *Willing to Believe*, pp. 15–27

2

Free Will and Divine Sovereignty

MESSAGE INTRODUCTION

One of the most basic theological questions involved with the doctrine of free will is the relationship between the will of man and the sovereignty of God. Many people believe that there is an inherent contradiction between the two concepts. In this lesson, Dr. Sproul examines this relationship and explains why a correct understanding of each concept leaves no real contradiction.

LEARNING OBJECTIVES

1. To understand the issues involved in the relationship between man's free will and God's sovereignty.
2. To be able to explain why the relationship is better defined as a mystery than a contradiction.
3. To be able to define the theological concept of concurrence.

QUOTATIONS

Man, by his fall into a state of sin, hath wholly lost all ability of will to any spiritual good accompanying salvation: so as, a natural man, being altogether averse from that good, and dead in sin, is not able, by his own strength, to convert himself, or to prepare himself thereunto.

—The Westminster Confession of Faith, Ch. IX:3

Although the will is free, this does not prevent its being determined by God and being always under subjection to him. This is so because liberty is not absolute, independent and uncontrolled (adespotos) (the characteristics of God alone), but limited and dependent.

—Francis Turretin

LECTURE OUTLINE

I. Introduction

  A. There are two fronts in the battle over free will:

    a. The relationship between free will and external power.

    b. The effects of sin upon moral freedom.

  B. The Biblical view of freedom contradicts all pagan notions of determinism, which reject God and see man as the supreme being, albeit one who remains a slave to the blind forces of nature.

II. The relationship between free will and divine sovereignty

  A. The larger theological question asks how free will is related to divine sovereignty.

  B. If God ordains today what is going to happen tomorrow, is there any question that what He has ordained will, in fact, come to pass? Or do we understand foreordination as an educated guess?

  C. If God knows that something is going to happen, it is absolutely certain to happen. It cannot not happen. But does that mean that God forces it to happen?

  D. Does foreordination carry the idea of predetermining what is going to come to pass?

III. Contradiction or mystery?

  A. Some argue that the concepts of free will and divine sovereignty are inherently contradictory.

  B. The relationship between the two concepts can be described as a mystery, but not as a contradiction.

  C. What are contradictory are divine sovereignty and human autonomy, or absolute freedom. These two concepts cannot be reconciled.

  D. The Bible nowhere teaches that human freedom is equivalent to autonomy.

  E. The Bible instead teaches that Adam's chief sin was the quest for autonomy, the desire to increase his real freedom to absolute freedom.

IV. Limited free will

  A. Some argue that God is sovereign, but that His sovereignty is limited by human freedom.

  B. If God's sovereignty is limited by man's freedom, then man is actually sovereign.

  C. Scripture teaches the opposite—that man's freedom is real, but that it is limited by the greater freedom of God.

  D. The concept of concurrence means that God works out His sovereignty—His supreme freedom—in, by, and through the real choices of His creatures, but in such a way that His creatures are not forced to act.

  E. The concept of intentionality means that human wills do actually function, but they are subject to the real supreme authority of God.

  F. Human beings are, at best, secondary causal agents.

STUDY QUESTIONS

1. The Biblical view of freedom contradicts all pagan notions of ____________.
   a. Determinism
   b. Divine sovereignty
   c. Predestination
   d. Salvation

2. If God knows that something is going to happen, it is ____________ happen.
   a. Probably not going to
   b. Undetermined whether it will
   c. Likely to
   d. Absolutely certain to

3. The relationship between the concepts of human free will and divine sovereignty can be described as ____________, but not as a contradiction.
   a. A mystery
   b. A logical incongruity
   c. An inconsistency
   d. A conundrum

4. There is a true contradiction between the concepts of divine sovereignty and human ____________.
   a. Free will
   b. Justice
   c. Autonomy
   d. Sanctification

5. If God's sovereignty is limited by man's freedom, then ____________ is actually sovereign.
   a. God
   b. Man
   c. No one
   d. Everyone

6. The concept of ____________ means that God works out His sovereignty—His supreme freedom—in, by, and through the real choices of His creatures, but in such a way that His creatures are not forced to act.
   a. Concurrence
   b. Intentionality
   c. Concupiscence
   d. Intelligibility

7. The concept of ____________ means that human wills do actually function, but they are subject to the real supreme authority of God.
   a. Freedom
   b. Autonomy
   c. Concurrence
   d. Intentionality

8. Human beings are, at best, ____________ causal agents.
   a. Primary
   b. Passive
   c. Secondary
   d. Unwilling

BIBLE STUDY

1. Read Ephesians 1:11. What things does God work according to the counsel of His will?

2. If God predestines all things, is man responsible for his actions? Read Luke 22:22. How does this passage of Scripture shed light on this question?

3. Read Genesis 50:20. How is the doctrine of concurrence illustrated by this verse?

4. Read Acts 2:23 and 4:27–28. How is the crucifixion of Christ said to be both the predetermined plan of God and an evil act of certain men?

5. Examine Romans 9:10–21. How does Paul expect many people to respond to the doctrine of God's sovereignty? What is Paul's response?

DISCUSSION QUESTIONS

1. Explain the doctrine of concurrence. Provide Scriptural examples.
2. What are some of the difficult questions raised in connection with the discussion of divine sovereignty and human free will? Which of these difficulties seem to be due to misunderstandings of the terms involved and which seem to be real mysteries?
3. Some have argued that human freedom can be maintained by suggesting that God foreordains only that which He foreknows. In other words, God looks into the future to see what His free creatures will choose to do, then foreordains those things to happen. Does this way of explaining human freedom remove the difficulties? Why or why not?
4. Is God related to time in the same way He is related to space? In other words, since time is part of creation, is God "omnitemporal" in relation to time in the same way

He is omnipresent in relation to space? If God were related to time in this way, would concepts such as "predestination" and "foreordination" have to be considered anthropomorphisms?

APPLICATION

1. How can a better understanding of God's sovereignty increase your faith and trust in Him?
2. Has this lesson answered any difficult questions you had regarding human free will and divine sovereignty? What new questions has it raised?
3. Do you ever fall into a way of thinking in which luck or chance plays a role in your life? Would a conscious effort at thankful prayer help to overcome that tendency?
4. Meditate on the text of Acts 2 (especially v. 23). Consider the mystery involved here. Examine what the text says about God predetermining the Crucifixion. Examine what the text says about the real sin and the real responsibility of the men who carried out the crucifixion of Jesus.

FOR FURTHER STUDY

Sproul, R.C. *Willing to Believe*, pp. 27–29

3

Are We Born Free?

MESSAGE INTRODUCTION

The long-standing dispute in the church over the relationship between the doctrines of original sin and free will emerged early in the Pelagian controversy. This controversy, which peaked in the late fourth and early fifth centuries, revolved around the writings of Pelagius and Augustine. In this lecture, Dr. Sproul introduces the main personalities, themes, and results of this controversy.

LEARNING OBJECTIVES

1. To be able to explain Pelagius' concerns and doctrine.
2. To be able to explain Augustine's concerns and doctrine.
3. To understand why the Gospel is at stake in this controversy.

QUOTATIONS

We, who have been instructed through the grace of Christ and born again to better manhood, . . . ought to be better than those who were before the law, and better than those who were under the law.

—Pelagius

It is humanity's fault that humanity is sinful. By the human will alone, humanity has fallen into a necessity of sinning which cannot be overcome by the human will alone.

—Augustine

LECTURE OUTLINE

I. Introduction

  A. The controversy over the relationship between original sin and free will emerged early in the history of the church with the Pelagian controversy.
  B. The controversy reached its peak at the end of the fourth and the beginning of the fifth centuries.
  C. In A.D. 418, at the Council of Carthage, Pelagius was condemned as a heretic.

II. Pelagius

  A. Pelagius was a zealous monk who traveled to Rome, where he was bothered by the licentiousness, godlessness, and cavalier attitude of Christians.
  B. He was provoked by a famous prayer of Augustine, in which Augustine had asked God to "grant what Thou commandest and command what Thou dost desire."
  C. Pelagius disagreed vehemently with the first half of the prayer. He said that if God commands man to do something, He doesn't have to grant him the power to do what He commands.
  D. According to Pelagius, whatever God commands imposes an obligation upon the creatures to obey, and since God is just, He would not and could not command His creatures to do something they are unable to do.
  E. Pelagius argued that God would be unjust if He were to command something beyond the ability of His creatures.
  F. The idea that man requires grace or assistance to do his duty was utterly repugnant to Pelagius.

III. Augustine

  A. According to Augustine, man cannot obey the law without grace because man is fallen, and the Fall involved the loss of moral power.
  B. God's law, His commands, cannot change. For God to command less than perfect holiness would be for God to command sin.
  C. Augustine was assuming the reality of the Fall and its consequences.
  D. The dispute turned into a controversy over the Fall and its effects on man's nature.

IV. The Pelagian controversy

  A. Pelagius did not deny that Adam sinned. Adam was created good and had the freedom and power to obey or disobey.
  B. But according to Pelagius, Adam's choice to sin did not change his nature, so every human being is born in the same moral condition that Adam was in before the Fall.
  C. According to Pelagius, man always has the ability to do good or evil.
  D. Pelagius argued that Adam's fall affected only Adam. There is no imputation of guilt or corruption of human nature as a result of the Fall.

E. Pelagius was not opposed to grace, but grace in his view facilitates obedience or righteousness. With grace it is easier to obey; grace helps but is not essential.
F. According to Pelagius, human beings can live perfect lives, and many have done so without grace.
G. Augustine responded that the human race is a mass of perdition, that no one can live a perfect life, and that even our good deeds are tainted by sin.

V. The Pelagian controversy and the Gospel
A. The whole concept of salvation is at stake in this controversy.
B. Pelagianism paves the way for pure legalism and self-righteousness.
C. According to Pelagius, the chief way in which Christ works on behalf of our redemption is by providing a good moral example.
D. Augustine saw Pelagius' doctrine as an attack on the heart of salvation and redemption.

STUDY QUESTIONS

1. In A.D. 418, at the Council of ____________, Pelagius was condemned as a heretic.
   a. Constantinople
   b. Carthage
   c. Chalcedon
   d. Nicea

2. Pelagius was a zealous ____________ who traveled to Rome, where he was bothered by the licentiousness, godlessness, and cavalier attitude of Christians.
   a. Archbishop
   b. Monk
   c. Pope
   d. Evangelist

3. Pelagius was provoked by something Augustine had said in a ____________.
   a. Book
   b. Prayer
   c. Commentary
   d. Funeral oration

4. According to ____________, man cannot obey the law without grace because man is fallen, and the Fall involved the loss of moral power.
   a. Semi-Pelagianism
   b. The Council of Trent
   c. Pelagius
   d. Augustine

5. The dispute turned into a controversy over ____________ and its effects on man's nature.
   a. The Fall
   b. Grace
   c. Lust
   d. Predestination

6. Pelagius argued that Adam's fall affected ____________.
   a. Adam and Eve
   b. Only Adam
   c. All mankind
   d. Only Cain

7. According to Pelagius, ____________ can live perfect lives.
   a. Those who hate God
   b. No human beings
   c. Some human beings
   d. All human beings

8. What is at stake in the Pelagian controversy is ____________.
   a. An insignificant issue
   b. Salvation
   c. The doctrine of supralapsarianism
   d. Justice

BIBLE STUDY

1. What do the following verses of Scripture say about the state in which natural man is born?
   a. Psalm 51:5
   b. Psalm 58:3

2. What do the following passages of Scripture say or imply about the spiritual state of the unregenerate man?
   a. Genesis 2:16–17
   b. Romans 5:12
   c. Ephesians 2:1–3
   d. Colossians 2:13

3. Read the following verses of Scripture. What do they tell us about the state of the natural man's heart?
   a. Genesis 8:21
   b. Ecclesiastes 9:3
   c. Jeremiah 17:9

d. Mark 7:21–23
e. John 3:19
f. Romans 8:7–8
g. 1 Corinthians 2:14
h. Ephesians 4:17–19
i. Ephesians 5:8
j. Titus 1:15

4. What do the following passages of Scripture say about the control of sin over the natural man?
   a. John 8:34, 44
   b. Romans 6:20
   c. Ephesians 2:1–2
   d. 2 Timothy 2:25–26
   e. Titus 3:3
   f. 1 John 3:10
   g. 1 John 5:19

5. What do the following Scripture passages teach us about the inherent ability of the natural man to repent and believe?
   a. Job 14:4
   b. Jeremiah 13:23
   c. Matthew 7:16–18
   d. Matthew 12:33
   e. John 6:44, 65
   f. 1 Corinthians 2:14
   g. 1 Corinthians 4:7
   h. 2 Corinthians 3:5
   i Ephesians 2:8

DISCUSSION QUESTIONS

1. Explain the concerns that led Pelagius to make the statements he made. Are his concerns legitimate? Do they necessitate the Pelagian answer?
2. What were Augustine's concerns? Why did he believe Pelagius' doctrine was an attack on the Gospel itself?
3. How did different views of the Fall significantly affect the respective views of Pelagius and Augustine? What are some other seemingly peripheral doctrines that could have a major impact upon our understanding of God, of Christ, and of the Gospel itself?

APPLICATION

1. What is your response when you hear Augustine's prayer to God to "grant what Thou commandest and command what Thou dost desire"?
2. Do you sympathize more with the concerns of Pelagius or Augustine? How has this lesson helped you understand the potential implications of your ideas?
3. Does Scripture support Pelagius' understanding of the natural man's abilities?

FOR FURTHER STUDY

Sproul, R.C. *Willing to Believe*, pp. 33–45

4

The Loss of Liberty

MESSAGE INTRODUCTION

Augustine of Hippo was the greatest theologian of the first thousand years of the church, and his controversy with Pelagius was one of the most important debates in the entire history of the church. The controversy established the framework for theological debate on the subject. In this lesson, Dr. Sproul examines Augustine's contribution to the Christian doctrine of free will.

LEARNING OBJECTIVES

1. To understand the basic distinction between free will and liberty as taught by Augustine.
2. To be able to define the Augustinian doctrine of freedom.
3. To be able to explain the difference in man's abilities before and after the Fall.

QUOTATIONS

I am, moreover, fully persuaded that the soul has fallen into sin, not through the fault of God, nor through any necessity either in the divine nature or in its own, but by its own free will; and that it can be delivered from the body of this death neither by the strength of its own will, as if that were in itself sufficient to achieve this, nor by the death of the body itself, but only by the grace of God through our Lord Jesus Christ, and that there is not one soul in the human family to whose salvation the one Mediator between God and man, the man Christ Jesus, is not absolutely necessary.

—Augustine

There is always within us a free will, but it is not always good. For it is either free from the control of righteousness when it serves sin—and then it is an evil will; or else it is free from the control of sin when it serves righteousness—and then it is a good will. But the grace of God is always good; and it is by grace that a human being comes to have a good will, though previously he had an evil one.

—Augustine

LECTURE OUTLINE

I. Introduction

A. Augustine made an important distinction during the Pelagian controversy between *liberum arbitrium* (free will) and *libertas* (liberty).

B. Augustine said that after the Fall man still had free will, but he had lost his liberty.

II. The effects of the Fall

A. Man was created as both a rational creature and a volitional creature.

B. The Fall affected the whole of man's nature.

C. The noetic effect of sin refers to the way the Fall affected man's mind, darkening and clouding it. It does not mean that the faculty of thought no longer exists; man still can think and reason.

D. In a similar way, although the Fall has done serious damage to our volition, it has not destroyed our will.

E. Man still makes choices. He still has a will that is free in the sense that it is not coerced by any external agency or power.

III. The concept of freedom

A. "Freedom" is a confusing term.

B. In the eighteenth century, it was understood to mean the freedom to do something.

C. Franklin Roosevelt used it to mean freedom *from* certain things.

D. Augustine said that fallen man's free will still has the ability to make choices according to its own desires; now, however, the will is in a state of corruption.

E. We are still free to do what we want, but the problem lies in what we want.

F. Man has lost any innate desire to seek God, please God, or have God in his thoughts. Man has a reprobate mind.

G. What man now lacks is liberty—the freedom to do or choose good as well as evil.

H. Augustine expressed the difference in the condition of pre-Fall man and post-Fall man with the following terms:

i. Pre-Fall man—*posse peccare* (the ability to sin) and *posse non peccare* (the ability to not sin). Pelagius taught that this condition remains after the Fall.

ii. Post-Fall man—*non posse non peccare* (the inability to not sin). This is the moral condition of original sin.

I. Pre-Fall man did not have *non posse peccare* (the inability to sin).

J. After the Fall, man was left in a state of moral inability. He does not have the power to choose God by himself because he does not have the desire to choose God.

STUDY QUESTIONS

1. The Latin term *liberum arbitrium* means ________________.
   a. Liberty
   b. Free will
   c. Autonomous liberty
   d. Arbitrary sovereignty

2. The Latin term *libertas* means ________________.
   a. Sovereignty
   b. Autonomy
   c. Liberty
   d. Free will

3. When theologians say that the Fall affected man's mind, darkening and clouding it, they are referring to the ____________ effects of sin.
   a. Noetic
   b. Mental
   c. Psychological
   d. Hypochondriacal

4. In the ____________ century, "freedom" was understood to mean the freedom to do something.
   a. Fifteenth
   b. Sixteenth
   c. Seventeenth
   d. Eighteenth

5. The Latin term for the ability to sin is ________________.
   a. *Non posse non peccare*
   b. *Non posse peccare*
   c. *Posse peccare*
   d. *Posse non peccare*

6. The Latin term for the ability to not sin is ________________.
   a. *Non posse non peccare*
   b. *Non posse peccare*
   c. *Posse peccare*
   d. *Posse non peccare*

7. The Latin term for the inability to not sin is ________________.
   a. *Non posse non peccare*
   b. *Non posse peccare*
   c. *Posse peccare*
   d. *Posse non peccare*

8. The Latin term for the inability to sin is ________________.
   a. *Non posse non peccare*
   b. *Non posse peccare*
   c. *Posse peccare*
   d. *Posse non peccare*

BIBLE STUDY

1. In John 8:43–44, what does Jesus say about the ability of unbelievers to hear His word?

2. Read Romans 6:17 and 6:20. How does Paul speak of the state of the Roman Christians before they were believers?

3. In Matthew 7:17–18, Jesus uses an illustration to describe the natural man's ability to do good. What does He say? What are the implications of His comments

4. How does Paul describe the state of unbelievers in Ephesians 2:1?

5. Read Romans 8:7–8. What does Paul say about the carnal mind's ability to be subject to the law of God?

6. Read 1 Corinthians 2:14. What does Paul say about the natural man's ability to receive and know the things of God?

DISCUSSION QUESTIONS

1. Read Romans 5:12–21. How do these verses describe the effects of Adam's sin on his posterity? How are these effects paralleled by the effects of Christ's work?
2. How does Augustine explain the implications of the difference between free will and liberty? How is this significant for understanding the Fall's effects on man's will?
3. Explain Augustine's description of the moral condition of pre-Fall and post-Fall man.

APPLICATION

1. How has this lesson helped you to better understand the nature of free will in relation to original sin?
2. Think through Augustine's explanation of man's ability before and after the Fall. How do the distinctions he made help us to better understand our own position in relation to God's grace?
3. Why is it important for you to understand that before you believed you were dead in sin, enslaved to sin, and completely unable to desire God?

FOR FURTHER STUDY

Sproul, R.C. *Willing to Believe*, pp. 49–66

5

Sovereign Grace

MESSAGE INTRODUCTION

The relationship between our desires and our choices is one of the key issues in the ongoing debate over free will. We do the things we do because we want to do them. The problem for the unregenerate man is that he does not want or desire God. He cannot choose that which he does not want to choose. In this lesson, Dr. Sproul explains the importance of understanding the relationship between our desires and our free choices.

LEARNING OBJECTIVES

1. To be able to explain the significance of Paul's doctrine of spiritual death.
2. To understand the difference between self-determination and determinism.
3. To be able to explain how fallen man can achieve liberty.

QUOTATIONS

Can sinners do anything good by the free determination of their own will? Again I say, God forbid. For it was by the evil use of his free will that man destroyed both it and himself. For, as a man who kills himself must, of course, be alive when he kills himself, but after he has killed himself ceases to live, and cannot restore himself to life; so, when man by his own free will sinned, then sin being victorious over him, the freedom of his will was lost.

—Augustine

A slave is freely in bondage if he does the will of his master with pleasure. Accordingly, he who is the servant of sin is free to sin. But he will not be free to do right, until he is set free from sin, and begins to be the servant of righteousness. And this is true liberty, for he now has pleasure in the righteous deed; and it is at the same time a holy bondage, for he is obedient to the will of God. But what is the origin of this liberty to do right for the person who is in bondage and sold under sin? He must be redeemed by Him who has said, "If the Son sets you free, you shall be free indeed" (John 8:36).

—Augustine

LECTURE OUTLINE

I. Introduction

A. There is an element of irony or paradox in Augustine's thought.
B. According to Augustine, we are in bondage to sin, but we are freely in bondage.
C. In the New Testament, Paul refers to himself as a bondservant of Christ.
D. The Greek word translated "bondservant" means a slave who was purchased.
E. Paul is a slave to Christ, yet he rejoices in his freedom in Christ.
F. The irony is that we must become slaves of God before we can experience the zenith of human freedom.

II. Dead or alive

A. In Ephesians 2:1ff, Paul writes to believers, "And you He made alive, who were dead in trespasses and sins. . . ."
B. When Paul speaks of the natural condition of fallen man, he speaks of spiritual death.
C. Augustine explained that man is biologically alive but spiritually dead.

III. Freedom or determinism

A. We do the things we do because we want to do them more than we don't want to do them.
B. We choose according to our desires; that is, we always do what we want to do.
C. Not only can we choose according to our strongest desire, but we must and always do choose according to our strongest desire at the moment.
D. This does not destroy freedom but instead establishes it, because free will is the ability to do what we want.
E. Freedom means self-determination, while determinism means external coercion.
F. This does not mean that our choices are utterly spontaneous and undetermined; our choices are determined by our desires—hence, self-determination.

IV. Moral ability

A. The big issue is how a person can achieve liberty—the moral ability to choose what is good, to choose the things of God.
B. Since fallen man is spiritually dead, he is a slave to himself, to his passions and lusts; he follows the desires of his evil heart.
C. According to Augustine, the liberation of fallen humanity absolutely requires God's grace.
D. Grace is a necessary condition of liberty.
E. In Ephesians 2:8, Paul writes, "For by grace you have been saved through faith, and that not of yourselves; it is the gift of God. . . ."

F. What is the antecedent of "it"? What is the gift of God?
G. Faith is the gift of God; it is an ability that fallen man does not have.
H. The whole of redemption is God's work alone because redemption requires that man be raised from the dead.
I. God alone can raise someone from death—whether biological or spiritual.

STUDY QUESTIONS

1. The Greek word translated "bondservant" means ____________.
   a. An employee
   b. A hired helper
   c. A squire
   d. A slave

2. The irony of Augustine's thought is that we must become ____________ before we can experience the zenith of human freedom.
   a. A slave of sin
   b. A slave of God
   c. Autonomous
   d. Coerced by an external force

3. When Paul speaks of the natural condition of fallen man, he speaks of spiritual ____________.
   a. Life
   b. Death
   c. Sickness
   d. Sleep

4. We choose according to ____________.
   a. Our desires
   b. That which we do not wish to do
   c. Deterministic factors
   d. Physical stimuli

5. "Free will" is defined as ____________.
   a. A myth
   b. The ability to do anything
   c. The ability to do what we want
   d. A Pelagian heresy

6. "Freedom" means ____________.
   a. Self-will
   b. Autonomy
   c. Coercion
   d. Self-determination

7. "Determinism" means _____________.
    a. Autonomy
    b. External coercion
    c. Free will
    d. Self-determination

8. _____________ is a necessary condition of liberty.
    a. Grace
    b. Autonomy
    c. The ability to do anything
    d. Determinism

BIBLE STUDY

1. Read Ephesians 2:1. What does Paul say that God did to the Ephesian believers? What was the previous state of the Ephesian believers?

2. Read Ephesians 2:2–3. How does Paul describe the former lives of the Ephesians?

3. Read Ephesians 2:4–7. According to Paul, what did God do for believers? According to verse 6, what has God already done for Christians? According to verse 7, what will God do for Christians.

4. Read Ephesians 2:8–9. How have we been saved? Did we accomplish it? How are salvation and faith described by Paul? Why does Paul say that salvation is not of works?

5. Read Ephesians 2:10. What were Christians created for in Christ Jesus, according to Paul? Does this contradict what Paul says in verse 9?

DISCUSSION QUESTIONS

1. What are some of the implications of viewing fallen man as spiritually dead? How does our view of the spiritual state of fallen man affect our view of redemption and the Gospel?
2. Explain how the fact that our choices are determined by our desires establishes rather than destroys human free will.
3. Read and meditate upon Ephesians 2:8–10. How does Paul relate good works to the gift of salvation?
4. Do you agree with Dr. Sproul's statement that "we always do what we want to do"? Why or why not?

APPLICATION

1. How conscious are you of having been spiritually dead prior to regeneration? How do you incorporate this fact before God in prayer?
2. What does it mean to you as a Christian to understand that every aspect of salvation, including your faith itself, is a gift from God?
3. Are you coerced to sin? Do you do so because you want to sin more than you want to please Christ at the moment of temptation? What are some things you can do to overcome these temptations?

FOR FURTHER STUDY

Sproul, R.C. *Commentary on Ephesians*

6

Is Grace Irresistible?

MESSAGE INTRODUCTION

The debate surrounding man's moral ability did not end with the condemnation of Pelagius. In southern France, there was a reaction against Augustine's doctrine. This reaction, which was spearheaded by a man named John Cassian, later became known as Semi-Pelagianism. In this lesson, Dr. Sproul explains the nature of this objection to Augustinianism.

LEARNING OBJECTIVES

1. To understand the background of the debate over Semi-Pelagianism.
2. To be able to explain the differences between Semi-Pelagianism and Pelagianism.
3. To be able to explain the differences between Semi-Pelagianism and Augustinianism.

QUOTATIONS

Everything that is commanded to human beings by the Lord in the holy Scriptures, for the sake of testing human free will, is either something we begin to obey by God's goodness, or is demanded in order to show us our need of grace to do it. Indeed, a person does not even begin to be changed from evil to good by the first stirrings of faith, unless the free and gratuitous mercy of God produces this in him. . . .

—Augustine

True liberty is also real health, and this would never have been lost if the will had remained good. But because the will has sinned, a harsh necessity of sinning will pursue the sinner, until his sickness is completely healed. When his freedom is fully regained, he will enjoy a permanent will to live happily. . . .

—Augustine

LECTURE OUTLINE

I. Introduction

   A. After the Pelagian controversy was officially settled, more objections were raised against Augustine.
   B. The reaction was centered in southern France in the rise of Semi-Pelagianism.
   C. The leader was John Cassian, who wrote 12 books in response to Augustine.
   D. Semi-Pelagianism is sometimes referred to as Cassianism.

II. The Semi-Pelagian debate

   A. Cassian's principal concern was predestination.
   B. He wanted to be able to advocate the universality of God's grace and say that man still has some ability to obey.
   C. Historically, Pelagianism has been regarded as an un-Christian and anti-Christian theology because it rejects the idea of the Fall.
   D. The debate over Semi-Pelagianism, which continues today, has been regarded as an intramural debate between Christians.
   E. Augustine claimed that God's grace is selective (e.g., Rom. 9); in other words, it is given to some but not to all.
   F. According to Cassian, Augustine's doctrine cripples the force of preaching and evangelism, and results in a kind of fatalism.

III. Semi-Pelagianism vs. Pelagianism

   A. Semi-Pelagianism is very different from Pelagianism.
   B. According to Pelagianism, there was no real Fall.
   C. Semi-Pelagianism teaches that there was a real Fall, that all men have become corrupt, that the will of man has become severely weakened, and that man cannot come to God apart from grace.
   D. But according to Semi-Pelagianism, man is not so dead that he has no moral ability; he still has the ability to cooperate or not cooperate with grace.
   E. Semi-Pelagianism teaches that God desires to save all men; that He gives grace to all men; and that the end result is determined by man's choice to cooperate or not cooperate.
   F. Semi-Pelagianism is the dominant position in the church today.

IV. Augustinianism vs. Semi-Pelagianism

   A. Augustine denied that fallen man has any power to cooperate.
   B. The issue is whether regeneration is monergistic or synergistic.
      i. *Monergism* means "one party working."
      ii. *Synergism* means "cooperation," or "more than one party working."
   C. Semi-Pelagianism teaches a synergistic view: that the effects of grace are determined by our willingness to cooperate with it.
   D. Augustine taught that regeneration and the effects of grace are the work of the Holy Spirit alone.

E. The debate also demonstrated the different views of predestination.
   i. Augustinianism: God decreed to save certain individuals.
   ii. Semi-Pelagianism: Predestination is based on God's foreknowledge.
F. Semi-Pelagianism was officially condemned at the Synod of Orange in A.D. 529.
G. Interestingly, the Catholic Church condemned Pelagianism, then it condemned Semi-Pelagianism, and in the sixteenth century it seems to have condemned Augustinianism.

STUDY QUESTIONS

1. The leader of the Semi-Pelagian movement was ____________, who wrote 12 books in response to Augustine.
   a. John Cassian
   b. Eusebius
   c. John Chrysostom
   d. Athanasius

2. Semi-Pelagianism is sometimes referred to as ____________.
   a. Eusebianism
   b. Semi-Augustinianism
   c. Cassianism
   d. Free-Will Theism

3. ____________ is the dominant position in the church today.
   a. Augustinianism
   b. Semi-Pelagianism
   c. Semi-Augustinianism
   d. Pelagianism

4. ____________ means "one party working."
   a. Synergism
   b. Monergism
   c. Monophysitism
   d. Pelagianism

5. ____________ means "cooperation," or more than "one party working."
   a. Synergism
   b. Augustinianism
   c. Synaptic
   d. Synchronous

6. Semi-Pelagianism teaches a ____________ view: that the effects of grace are determined by our willingness to cooperate with it.
   a. Non-Christian
   b. Dualistic
   c. Monergistic
   d. Synergistic

7. According to Semi-Pelagianism, predestination is based on ____________.
   a. God's will
   b. Election
   c. God's foreknowledge
   d. Synergism

8. Semi-Pelagianism was officially condemned at the ____________ in A.D. 529.
   a. Diet of Worms
   b. Synod of Orange
   c. Council of Chalcedon
   d. Council of Carthage

BIBLE STUDY

1. Examine Romans 9:10–18 closely.
   a. Was God's choice of Jacob over Esau based on any good or evil foreseen in them?
   b. On what basis does God show mercy, and on what basis does He harden hearts?

2. According to Jesus in John 15:16, whose choice is primary, God's or man's?

3. Read Ephesians 1:3–6.
   a. When did God choose those whom He would save?
   b. On what basis was His choice made?
   c. For what purpose was His choice made?

4. Read Philippians 1:29. Does Paul in this verse describe the origin or source of belief in Christ as coming from God or man?

DISCUSSION QUESTIONS

1. Explain the principal teachings of Augustine that caused John Cassian difficulty. Why did Cassian have problems with these doctrines? Do you hear these same objections raised today? Are they valid concerns?
2. Outline some of the more important differences between Semi-Pelagianism and Pelagianism. What are some of the reasons that Pelagianism is considered un-Christian while Semi-Pelagianism is considered to be Christian?

3. Explain the central points of Augustine's response to Semi-Pelagianism, especially as it relates to regeneration.
4. What do you think are the main reasons that Semi-Pelagianism is the dominant position in the church today?

APPLICATION

1. Have you ever had any of the concerns expressed by John Cassian? How have your concerns been resolved?
2. How has this lesson affected your thinking about the role man plays in salvation?
3. Do you have difficulty accepting Paul's response to God's electing choice in Romans 9:20–21? Why is it important to bring your thinking and attitudes more in line with those of the apostle?

FOR FURTHER STUDY

Sproul, R.C. *Willing to Believe*, pp. 69–76

7

A Divided Will?

MESSAGE INTRODUCTION

The Roman Catholic Church faces an unusual problem in relation to Augustinianism. It has, at different points in its history, condemned Pelagianism, Semi-Pelagianism, and Augustinianism. It has condemned all of the options. Today, it has adopted a form of Semi-Pelagianism. In this lesson, Dr. Sproul explains the historic controversy over Augustinianism in the Roman Catholic church.

LEARNING OBJECTIVES

1. To understand the modern Roman Catholic Church's stand on Semi-Pelagianism.
2. To be able to outline the main points in the doctrine of irresistible grace.
3. To be able to outline the main personalities and points in the Jansenist controversy.

QUOTATIONS

If anyone contends that God waits for our decision to cleanse us from sin and does not confess that the bestowal of the Spirit and his action in us moves us to will to be cleansed, he opposes this Holy Spirit. . . .

—Synod of Orange

If anyone says that man's free will [when] moved and roused by God, by assenting to God . . . in no way cooperates toward disposing and preparing itself to obtain the grace of justification. . . [and] that it cannot refuse its assent if it wishes, . . . let him be anathema!

—Council of Trent

LECTURE OUTLINE

I. Introduction

   A. The Roman Catholic Church faces a problem because of a built-in ambiguity in its theological system.
   B. In the fifth century, the church condemned Pelagianism; it then condemned Semi-Pelagianism in A.D. 529.
   C. It appears that the Roman Church also repudiated the Augustinian view at the time of the Reformation.
   D. It seems that all of the soteriological options have been condemned at one time or another by the Roman Catholic Church.

II. Modern Roman Catholicism and Semi-Pelagianism

   A. The Roman Catholic Church today has reverted back to a form of Semi-Pelagianism.
   B. At the Council of Trent, the first three canons repeated the church's condemnation of Pelagianism.
   C. Canon four of the sixth session seemed to be aimed directly at the Reformers: "If anyone says that man's free will . . . in no way cooperates toward disposing and preparing itself to obtain the grace of justification . . . let him be anathema."
   D. According to Rome, the will must cooperate with the grace of God given in justification in order for man to be saved.
   E. The ambiguity lies in the phrase "grace of justification." Does Rome mean the grace of regeneration or a cooperation that takes place after regeneration?
   F. Canon four also condemns those who would say that the free will of man "cannot refuse its assent [to God's grace] if it wishes."

III. Irresistible grace

   A. The main point of the doctrine of irresistible (or effectual) grace is that when God changes the heart, the heart responds.
   B. It does not mean that grace is incapable of being resisted.
   C. The real question is whether grace is effective or whether it requires cooperation.
   D. The Reformers argued that grace changes the desires of the heart.
   E. Canon four of the Council of Trent condemned those who said that the free will was merely passive or inanimate, but Augustine and the Reformers never claimed that the free will was inanimate.
   F. The Reformers did say that the human spirit is utterly passive when God's regenerating grace meets the dead spirit of man.
   G. The human spirit, according to the Reformers, is passive until the Holy Spirit raises it from death; then it is no longer passive.

IV. Ongoing controversy

A. In the seventeenth century, the Roman Catholic Church condemned Michael Baius for teaching that the will without grace can only sin, that apart from regenerating grace the will is free only to sin.
B. Ironically, Baius' teaching was taken directly from Augustine.
C. The Jansenist controversy began when Cornelius Jansen wrote a book titled *Augustinus*, in which he basically reproduced the theology of Augustine.
D. In 1653, Pope Innocent X condemned five of the Jansenist theses:
    i. Some commandments of God are impossible for men to obey because they lack the grace that would make obedience possible.
    ii. Fallen men never resist inward grace.
    iii. Man does not require freedom from necessity, only freedom from coercion.
    iv. Prevenient grace is necessary for single acts, but this grace cannot be resisted.
    v. It is Semi-Pelagian to say that Christ died for all men.
E. Semi-Pelagianism is also evident in the *Catechism of the Catholic Church* (1994), which states that even after the Fall man still has the power of choosing evil or good.
F. In fact, some of the statements in the new catechism sound more Pelagian than Semi-Pelagian.

STUDY QUESTIONS

1. The Roman Catholic Church today has reverted back to a form of ______________.
    a. Semi-Augustinianism
    b. Pelagianism
    c. Semi-Pelagianism
    d. Eastern Orthodoxy

2. At the Council of Trent, the first three canons repeated the church's condemnation of ______________.
    a. Semi-Augustinianism
    b. Augustinianism
    c. Semi-Pelagianism
    d. Pelagianism

3. Irresistible grace is sometimes referred to as ______________ grace.
    a. Effectual
    b. Omnipotent
    c. Amazing
    d. Irresolute

4. In the seventeenth century, the Roman Catholic Church condemned ____________ for teaching that the will without grace can only sin, that apart from regenerating grace the will is free only to sin.
   a. William of Ockham
   b. John Cassian
   c. John Calvin
   d. Michael Baius

5. The Jansenist controversy began when ____________ wrote a book titled *Augustinus*.
   a. Jan Hus
   b. Cornelius Jansen
   c. Michael Jansen
   d. Jan Vincent

6. The Jansenist theses basically reproduced the theology of ____________.
   a. Augustine
   b. Pelagius
   c. John Cassian
   d. Michael Baius

7. In 1653, ____________ condemned five of the Jansenist theses.
   a. Pope Paul I
   b. The Council of Carthage
   c. Pope Innocent X
   d. The Council of Trent

8. ____________ is evident in the *Catechism of the Catholic Church.*
   a. Augustinianism
   b. Jansenism
   c. Supralapsarianism
   d. Semi-Pelagianism

BIBLE STUDY

1. Read John 1:12–13. According to John, those who become children of God are born of whose will?

2. What light does John 3:27 shed on the issue of divine sovereignty and human free will?

3. According to John 5:21, to whom does the Son give life?

4. Read Acts 16:14. How did Lydia come to believe in Christ? Was she able to believe by her own natural ability?

DISCUSSION QUESTIONS

1. Explain the problems involved with the Roman Catholic doctrine of the church's infallibility as it relates to the church's dogmatic statements concerning the ongoing controversy over free will.
2. Why is the doctrine of the Council of Trent on the subject of free will so ambiguous and difficult to understand? What specific statements made by the council are particularly difficult?
3. Define the doctrine of irresistible (or effectual) grace and explain its importance in the debate over free will.
4. Why were the Roman Catholic condemnations of Michael Baius and the Jansenist theses doctrinally problematic for the Roman church?

APPLICATION

1. Do you remember the first time you heard and responded to the Gospel? Do you believe the Holy Spirit was working to effectually call you? Why?
2. How does an understanding of irresistible grace change your understanding of how the Gospel should be presented?
3. Why is the evangelistic methodology that relies almost exclusively on persuasive techniques problematic? Have you used these techniques? Will you continue to do so after studying this lesson?

FOR FURTHER STUDY

Sproul, R.C. *Willing to Believe*, pp. 77–84

8

Bondage of the Will

MESSAGE INTRODUCTION

In the sixteenth century, a fascinating debate occurred between Martin Luther and Desiderius Erasmus. The subject of the debate was free will. Luther's response was published as a book titled The Bondage of the Will, which he considered to be his most important work. In this lecture, Dr. Sproul explains the background and the main issues of this debate.

LEARNING OBJECTIVES

1. To understand the crucial importance of the debate between Luther and Erasmus.
2. To be able to outline the main points advocated by Luther and Erasmus.
3. To be able to explain Luther's critique of Erasmus.

QUOTATIONS

If it is not in the power of every man to keep what is commanded, all the exhortations in the Scriptures, and all the promises, threats, expostulations, reproofs, adjurations, blessings, curses and hosts of precepts, are of necessity useless.

—Desiderius Erasmus

You describe the power of "free will" as small, and wholly ineffective apart from the grace of God. Agreed? Now then, I ask you: if God's grace is wanting, if it is taken away from that small power, what can it do? It is ineffective, you say, and can do nothing good. So it will not do what God or His grace wills. Why? Because we have now taken God's grace away from it, and what the grace of God does not do is not good. Hence it follows that "free will" without God's grace is not free at all, but is the permanent prisoner and bondslave of evil, since it cannot turn itself to good.

—Martin Luther

LECTURE OUTLINE

I. Introduction

A. In the sixteenth century, Martin Luther and Desiderius Erasmus engaged in one of the most fascinating debates in church history.
B. In 1524, Erasmus wrote *A Diatribe Concerning Free Will.*
C. In 1525, Luther responded with *The Bondage of the Will.*
D. Luther said this book was his most important work, and historians generally have agreed.
E. The battle cry of the Reformation was justification *sola fide*, "by faith alone."
F. But according to Luther, justification was only the tip of the iceberg; beneath the surface was the doctrine of *sola gratia*, "grace alone."
G. *Sola fide* depends on *sola gratia.*

II. The debate

A. Luther was an Augustinian monk influenced heavily by the namesake of his monastic order.
B. Erasmus argued that the whole issue of free will was an academic point that was not all that important.
C. Luther responded that the matter was of crucial importance, saying that the part God plays and the part we play in salvation have everything to do with our religious posture before God, our understanding and appreciation of the grace of God, and our worship of God.
D. Erasmus was concerned about some of the practical consequences that might flow out of Reformed teaching on moral inability and God's sovereignty; in this he shared the concerns of John Cassian.
E. Erasmus asked, "If we teach this doctrine, who will try to reform his life? Who will believe God loves him?"
F. Luther answered, "Nobody," and went on to say that is the crux of the problem: Nobody wants God.

III. Luther's critique of Erasmus

A. Luther asked, "If it all comes down to your willing or not willing, your rejecting or accepting, your choosing or not choosing to cooperate with the grace of God, then what is it in your fallen nature that will cause one to say yes and another to say no?"
B. There must be some kind of desire or inclination in the soul; we say yes or no because we want to, but the question is, "Why?"
C. According to Luther, if it is the human will, then the person has something to boast about.
D. Erasmus also complained about the doctrine of predestination, arguing that it necessarily entails coercion.
E. Luther said God doesn't force man to act.

STUDY QUESTIONS

1. In 1524, Erasmus wrote ____________.
   a. *A Diatribe Concerning Free Will*
   b. *A Diatribe Concerning the Bondage of the Will*
   c. *The Bondage of the Will*
   d. *The Freedom of the Will*

2. In 1525, Luther responded with ____________.
   a. *A Diatribe Concerning Free Will*
   b. *A Diatribe Concerning the Bondage of the Will*
   c. *The Bondage of the Will*
   d. *The Freedom of the Will*

3. Luther said this book was his most ____________ work, and historians generally have agreed.
   a. Pastoral
   b. Theological
   c. Important
   d. Practical

4. The battle cry of the Reformation was ____________.
   a. *Sola fide*
   b. *Sola Scriptura*
   c. "Onward, Christian Soldiers"
   d. *Semper reformanda*

5. According to the Reformers, *sola fide* depends on ____________.
   a. *Sola Scriptura*
   b. *Sola gratia*
   c. *Semper reformanda*
   d. *Soli Deo gloria*

6. Luther was ____________ monk influenced heavily by the namesake of his monastic order.
   a. An Augustinian
   b. A Benedictine
   c. A Cistercian
   d. A Franciscan

7. Erasmus argued that the whole issue of free will was ____________.
   a. Extremely significant
   b. Unjust
   c. An anthropomorphism
   d. Unimportant

8. Erasmus' concerns were essentially the same as those expressed earlier in history by ______________.
   a. Pelagius
   b. Augustine
   c. John Cassian
   d. Michael Baius

BIBLE STUDY

1. According to Jesus in John 6:44, who has the ability to come to Him? How does a person come to Him, according to the same verse?

2. How does Jesus describe the state of sinners in John 8:34? Is it a state of freedom or bondage?

3. Read Romans 3:9–18. How many people are under sin, according to Paul? How many seek after God?

4. Read Romans 8:7–8. Can the carnal mind be subject to the law of God? Do those in the flesh have the ability to please God?

DISCUSSION QUESTIONS

1. Explain why *sola fide* necessarily depends on *sola gratia.*
2. Explain the main points of dispute between Erasmus and Luther. Why were the main concerns of Erasmus a strength rather than a weakness of Reformed doctrine?
3. What was the main point of Luther's critique of Erasmus? How did Erasmus' doctrine compromise the Gospel, according to Luther?

APPLICATION

1. In the past, have you considered the debate over free will to be an unimportant academic debate? Has this lecture changed your opinion on the matter in any way? How?
2. Meditate on how *sola fide* rests on *sola gratia.* Has your understanding of the real meaning of *sola gratia* been clarified as this course has proceeded?
3. Many Protestants consider Martin Luther's *The Bondage of the Will* to be the most important book written at the time of the Reformation and a foundational book for Protestant theology. Determine to read this book at some point during the next year.

FOR FURTHER STUDY

Sproul, R.C. *Willing to Believe*, pp. 87–102
Luther, Martin. *The Bondage of the Will*

9

Voluntary Slaves

MESSAGE INTRODUCTION

In the public mind, John Calvin is the person most commonly associated with a denial of free will. In reality, there is nothing in Calvin's thought that is not found in the writings of Augustine. In this lecture, Dr. Sproul points out some of the common misconceptions about Calvin's theology and explains his concept of the will.

LEARNING OBJECTIVES

1. To be able to explain the Augustinian roots of Calvin's thought.
2. To be able to outline Calvin's position on the doctrines of total depravity, unconditional election, and regeneration.
3. To be able to explain the crucial importance of John 6:44 to a proper understanding of man's ability.

QUOTATIONS

When the will is enchained as the slave of sin, it cannot make a movement towards goodness, far less steadily pursue it. Every such movement is the first step in that conversion to God, which in Scripture is entirely ascribed to divine grace.

—John Calvin

Man, since he was corrupted by the fall, sins not forced or unwillingly, but voluntarily, by a most forward bias of the mind; not by violent compulsion, or external force, but by the movement of his own passion; and yet such is the depravity of his nature, that he cannot move and act except in the direction of evil.

—John Calvin

LECTURE OUTLINE

I. Introduction

A. In public thinking, no one is more clearly associated with a denial of free will than John Calvin.
B. Calvin was devoted to the study of Augustine.
C. In his writings, Calvin quotes Augustine far more than any other patristic writer.
D. There is nothing in Calvin's doctrine of free will that was not in the writings of Augustine and Luther.

II. Total depravity

A. "Total depravity" does not mean that man is as wicked as he possibly can be.
B. Rather, "total depravity" means that the totality of human nature and existence is depraved.
C. The Fall affected all of the human being—mind, heart, body, and will.
D. Man after the Fall is in a state of moral inability, but this does not mean that man cannot achieve civic virtue.
E. The corruption of the will pertains to the vertical dimension—the inclination to do and desire the things of God.

III. Unconditional election

A. When God elects, He does not do so on the basis of His prior knowledge of which individuals will meet His conditions.
B. If election were conditional upon fallen man's choice, no one would be elected because God would foresee no one's choosing Him.

IV. Regeneration

A. Regeneration is a necessary requirement for man to be liberated from bondage to sin.
B. The flesh will not incline itself to God without regeneration.
C. Man is unable to free himself by an exertion of his own will.
D. In the Fall, man did not lose the faculty of choosing any more than he lost the faculty of thinking. These two faculties were not destroyed but darkened.
E. Man was not deprived of will in the Fall; he was deprived of liberty.

V. The inability of man

A. John 6:44 indicates that no one ever will come to Christ of himself.
B. John says, "'No one can come to Me unless the Father who sent Me draws him. . . .'"
   i. "No one" is a universal negative proposition.
   ii. "Can" means ability or power.
   iii. "Come to Me" is the specific ability in question.
   iv. "Unless" indicates a necessary condition.
   v. The condition is the drawing of the Father.

STUDY QUESTIONS

1. John Calvin was devoted to the study of ____________.
   a. Francis Turretin
   b. Augustine
   c. John Cassian
   d. Martin Luther

2. Who is quoted far more than any other patristic writer in Calvin's writings?
   a. Tertullian
   b. John Chrysostom
   c. Athanasius
   d. Augustine

3. "Total depravity" means ____________.
   a. Man is as bad as he possibly can be.
   b. The totality of human nature and existence is depraved.
   c. Man is no longer in the image of God.
   d. Certain aspects of man's nature have been affected by the Fall.

4. "Unconditional election" means that ____________.
   a. When God elects, He unconditionally elects Christ, and those who then choose to believe in Christ become elect.
   b. When God elects individuals to salvation, He does not do so on the condition of foreseen faith.
   c. When God elects, He does so on the basis of unconditional faithfulness that He foresees in an individual.
   d. When God elects, He does so on the basis of His prior knowledge of which individuals will meet his conditions.

5. If election were conditional upon fallen man's choice, how many would be elected?
   a. A vast majority
   b. Very few
   c. No one
   d. Everyone

6. ____________ is a necessary requirement for a person to be liberated from bondage to sin.
   a. Regeneration
   b. Total depravity
   c. Autonomy
   d. All of the above

7. The ____________ will not incline itself to God without regeneration.
   a. World
   b. Church
   c. Body
   d. Flesh

8. Man is ____________ to free himself by an exertion of the will.
   a. Able
   b. Able with assistance
   c. Unable
   d. None of the above

BIBLE STUDY

1. Read John 6:44. What do the words "no one" mean? How universal is this statement?

2. What does the word "can" mean? Why is the proper definition of this word crucial to a proper interpretation of this verse?

3. What does Jesus mean when He says "come to Me" in this verse? Who is able to do this, according to Christ?

4. The word "unless" has a specific meaning, according to Dr. Sproul. What does it mean?

5. How do the words "unless the Father who sent Me draws him" fit into the rest of the verse? What is the point of this statement by Jesus?

DISCUSSION QUESTIONS

1. What are some of the common caricatures of Calvin's teaching, and how do they compare to what Calvin actually taught?
2. Explain the Calvinist doctrine of total depravity. How does this doctrine affect one's doctrine of the will?
3. Using John 6:44, explain why regeneration is absolutely necessary for man to be able to come to God.

APPLICATION

1. Is it difficult for you to believe the doctrine of total depravity? Why do you believe this doctrine is so difficult for people to accept?
2. What misconceptions about Calvin's teaching has this lesson helped to clear up?
3. Can you think of any potential objections to the Calvinist interpretation of John 6:44?

FOR FURTHER STUDY

Sproul, R.C. *Willing to Believe*, pp. 105–122

Calvin, John. *The Bondage and Liberation of the Will*

10

Is Grace Cooperative?

MESSAGE INTRODUCTION

Something similar to the Semi-Pelagian controversy occurred in the sixteenth and seventeenth centuries in the Reformed church, when James Arminius objected to several elements of Calvinistic thought. In this lesson, Dr. Sproul exposes some of the misunderstandings surrounding Arminius' thought and explains the actual differences between Arminianism and Reformed theology.

LEARNING OBJECTIVES

1. To understand the background of the Arminian controversy.
2. To be able to outline the main Arminian objections to Calvinism.
3. To be able to outline the Reformed response to Arminius' main objection.

QUOTATIONS

All unregenerate persons have freedom of will, and a capability of resisting the Holy Spirit, of rejecting the proffered grace of God, . . . and of not opening to Him who knocks at the door of the heart; and these things they can actually do.

—James Arminius

Therefore, all people are conceived in sin and are born children of wrath, unfit for any saving good, inclined to evil, dead in their sins, and slaves to sin; without the grace of the regenerating Holy Spirit they are neither willing nor able to return to God, to reform their distorted nature, or even to dispose themselves to such reform.

—The Synod of Dordt

LECTURE OUTLINE

I. Introduction

A. The problem of straw-man arguments can be illustrated by considering the following quotation by James Arminius. In the fallen state, "the free will of man towards the true good is not only wounded, maimed, infirm, bent, and weakened; but it is also imprisoned, destroyed, and lost. And its powers are not only debilitated and useless unless they be assisted by grace, but it has no powers whatever except such as are excited by Divine grace."

B. Many Christians would have a hard time distinguishing the content of this quotation from the Reformed doctrine on the same subject.

C. Arminius was a Reformed theologian at the beginning of his career, but during a dispute over supralapsarianism he gradually moved away from Calvinism.

II. The doctrine of Arminius

A. Arminius taught that the Fall affected all three parts of human nature: the mind, the affections, and the will.

B. He taught that man is dead in sin, morally unable to do any good unless liberated by God.

C. He posited the working of preventing (or prevenient) grace—grace that comes before conversion and must do so for conversion to happen.

D. Some theologians argued that grace works only externally, but Arminius agreed with Augustine, Luther, and Calvin by saying that grace also works internally.

E. He differed from the Reformed theologians when he argued that although grace is internal, it is not irresistible.

III. Resistible grace

A. Arminius taught that fallen man needs the intrusion of internal grace, but in order to be converted, he must respond positively.

B. The grace of regeneration, according to Arminius, is sufficient to convert, but it is not inherently efficient—it does not always effect conversion.

C. The major contrast between Arminianism and Calvinism at this point is over the doctrine of effectual calling.

D. Arminius claimed that if man does not assent to grace, the responsibility rests exclusively with man.

E. Arminius' concern was with the justice of God. He argued that if God gives effectual grace only to some, then God gets both the credit for salvation and the blame for damnation.

F. He thought that his schema would allow him to say that blame for damnation lies with the individual, while the credit for salvation belongs to God alone.

G. But if rejection of grace is a fault, acceptance of grace must be a virtue, a good work.

IV. Analogies

A. Arminians have used a number of analogies to illustrate their teaching.
   i. A rich man freely bestows a valuable gift upon a beggar, offering all the beggar could hope for. All the beggar has to do is reach out and accept the gift, but he has the ability to refuse the gift.
   ii. A person with a fatal illness must simply accept the offer of a miracle cure in order to be completely healed.
   iii. A drowning man simply needs to reach out and grab the life preserver thrown to him.

B. The Reformed response has been to emphasize the point that the unsaved man is not drowning. He is dead and at the bottom of the ocean. He needs life, not a life preserver.

V. The Synod of Dordt

A. After Arminius died in 1609, his followers were involved in the Remonstrant controversy in the Netherlands.

B. They presented five objections to the official Reformed church's doctrine. They argued that:
   i. God's election is based on His foreknowledge.
   ii. Christ died for every individual.
   iii. Grace is utterly necessary for faith or any good deed.
   iv. Grace can be resisted.
   v. The perseverance of the saints is open to question.

C. In 1618, the Remonstrant controversy led to the Synod of Dordt, at which all five theses were rejected.

D. The Reformed doctrine was reaffirmed in terms of five points. These have become commonly known as the "five points of Calvinism."

STUDY QUESTIONS

1. James Arminius began his career as ______________ theologian.
   a. An Anabaptist
   b. A Lutheran
   c. A Roman Catholic
   d. A Reformed

2. Arminius posited the working of ______________ grace—grace that comes before conversion and must do so for conversion to happen.
   a. Subsequential
   b. Prevenient
   c. Prior
   d. Previous

3. According to Arminius, the grace of regeneration ____________.
   a. Does not always effect conversion
   b. Is irresistible
   c. Is unconditional
   d. Always effects conversion

4. The major contrast between Arminianism and Calvinism is over the doctrine of ____________.
   a. Effectual calling
   b. Christology
   c. The Holy Spirit's power
   d. Omnipotence

5. What was the controversy that erupted in the early seventeenth century between Arminians and Calvinists?
   a. The Synod of Dordt
   b. The Semi-Pelagian controversy
   c. The Remonstrant controversy
   d. The Council of Trent

6. Where did the controversy between the Arminians and Calvinists erupt?
   a. England
   b. Switzerland
   c. Germany
   d. The Netherlands

7. What was the name of the meeting that was held in 1618 to resolve the controversy between Arminianism and Calvinism?
   a. The Diet of Worms
   b. The Synod of Dordt
   c. The Westminster Assembly
   d. The Council of Trent

8. As a result of the Arminian/Calvinist controversy, the Reformed doctrine became commonly known as ____________.
   a. The five points of Calvinism
   b. Supralapsarianism
   c. Dordtism
   d. Augustinianism

BIBLE STUDY

1. Read Romans 8:30. Is calling an act of God or an act of man? What does God do for those whom He calls?

2. What does Paul say about God's calling in 1 Corinthians 1:9?

3. What light does Romans 1:6 shed on the doctrine of effectual calling?

4. How is God's effectual calling accomplished, according to 2 Thessalonians 2:14?

DISCUSSION QUESTIONS

1. Read the quotation by Arminius at the beginning of the outline for this lesson. Does the content of this statement contradict any doctrines you have heard attributed to Arminius? How important is it to accurately present the position of those with whom you disagree?
2. Explain Arminius' view on the effects of the Fall and on the workings of grace in man. How does this view differ from the Reformed Augustinian position?
3. Examine the analogies used by Arminius and his followers to explain the Gospel offer. How many of these have you heard used? What are their weaknesses? How could these weaknesses potentially obscure the graciousness of the Gospel?

APPLICATION

1. As you have proceeded through this study, have you discovered that you have been guilty of misrepresenting the views of any man or group? What can you do to prevent such a misrepresentation from occurring?
2. How many times did you hear the Gospel before God effectually called you through a human presentation of that Gospel? Do you remember the difference between that one time and the others?
3. Will you still be comfortable using the evangelistic illustrations that were described in this lesson after hearing of their origin and theological underpinnings? Why or why not?

FOR FURTHER STUDY

Sproul, R.C. *Willing to Believe*, pp. 125–143

11

Born to Sin?

MESSAGE INTRODUCTION

In 1754, a pastor in Northampton, Mass., wrote perhaps the most insightful book on the doctrine of human free will ever written. The pastor's name was Jonathan Edwards, and the book was titled On The Freedom of the Will. In this lecture, Dr. Sproul explains the importance of Edwards' work on the doctrine of the will.

LEARNING OBJECTIVES

1. To be able to outline Edwards' basic definition of the nature of the will.
2. To understand the role of desire in the action of the will.
3. To be able to explain why the concept of an uncaused choice is irrational.

QUOTATIONS

The faculty of the will is that faculty or power or principle of mind by which it is capable of choosing: an act of the will is the same as an act of choosing or choice.

—Jonathan Edwards

If the case be such indeed, that all mankind are by nature in a state of total ruin, . . . then, doubtless, the great salvation by Christ stands in direct relation to this ruin, as the remedy to the disease.

—Jonathan Edwards

LECTURE OUTLINE

I. Introduction

A. Jonathan Edwards was a pastor in Northampton, Mass., who left his church because of slander and became a minister to the Indians.

B. In 1754, Edwards published what is arguably his greatest work, *On the Freedom of the Will.*

II. The nature of the will

A. Edwards agreed that we must distinguish between the faculty of thinking and the faculty of choosing, but he warned against separating them.
B. He argued that the two faculties are intimately interrelated.
C. He defined the will as "the mind choosing."
D. Edwards looked at the problem in relation to the law of causality, which states that every effect must have a cause.
E. Since a human choice is an effect, it must have a cause, and the cause is found in the mind.
F. Choices are made for a reason; they are based on what we deem to be good for us, what is pleasing to us.

III. The role of desire in the action of the will

A. According to Edwards, the mind considers an action to be good, and on that basis a choice is made.
B. All choices are caused by inclinations.
C. We are complex beings with complex motives and conflicting desires, but we always and everywhere choose according to our strongest inclination at the moment.
D. Without an inclination, there wouldn't be a choice.
E. This is the essence of freedom: the ability to choose what one wants.

IV. Uncaused choice?

A. Edwards argued against those who said that man cannot be free unless the will is totally indifferent.
B. According to Edwards, an indifferent choice is an irrational concept for two reasons:
    i. If we make a choice for no reason, it would have no moral significance.
    ii. If there is no inclination, it is impossible to choose at all, because an effect without a cause is impossible.

V. Natural ability and moral ability

A. Fallen man has the natural ability to make choices and to be volitional.
B. Fallen man lacks the moral ability to choose the things of God.
C. Man lacks this moral ability because, in the Fall, he lost the disposition, desire, and inclination for God.
D. Man cannot choose God because he does not want to until and unless the Holy Spirit regenerates him.

STUDY QUESTIONS

1. Jonathan Edwards was a pastor in ____________.
   a. Philadelphia
   b. Boston
   c. Northampton, Mass.
   d. Charleston, S.C.

2. In 1754, Edwards published what is arguably his greatest work, ____________.
   a. *The Bondage of the Will*
   b. *On the Freedom of the Will*
   c. *On the Liberty of the Will*
   d. *On the Sovereign Will of God*

3. Edwards defined the will as ____________.
   a. "The mind choosing"
   b. "An indifferent chooser"
   c. "Desire"
   d. "An inclination"

4. According to Edwards, all choices are caused by ____________.
   a. Nothing
   b. Inclinations
   c. Environmental factors
   d. External coercion

5. We are complex beings with complex motives and conflicting desires, but we always and everywhere choose according to our ____________ at the moment.
   a. Predetermined fate
   b. Physical inclinations
   c. Faculties
   d. Strongest inclination

6. The essence of freedom is ____________.
   a. The ability to do anything
   b. Autonomy
   c. The ability to choose what one wants
   d. Liberation

7. If there is no inclination, choosing is ____________.
   a. Impossible
   b. Difficult
   c. Coerced
   d. An illusion

8. In the Fall, man lost his ____________.
   a. Moral ability
   b. Natural ability
   c. Inclinations
   d. Will

BIBLE STUDY

1. In Romans 6, we find a description of the state of slavery into which all men are born contrasted with the state of freedom into which Christians are re-born. Read Romans 6 and answer the following questions.
   a. In verses 1–7, Paul says that our old man was crucified with Christ. What is the result of this action? How is the believer now related to sin?
   b. In verses 12–14, Paul instructs believers on the basis of what he has said in verses 1–7. What does Paul tell believers here? What is the relationship of this instruction to the truths Paul already has communicated?
   c. What does Paul say is true of believers in verses 17–18? Are believers slaves? To what?
   d. How does Paul describe the state of slavery in verses 20–23? How does he contrast slavery to sin and slavery to God?

2. Read John 8:35–36. Who sets man free? Does man accomplish his own release from slavery to sin?

3. What do the following verses add to our understanding of slavery and freedom?
   a. 2 Corinthians 3:17
   b. Galatians 5:1

4. What do the following passages of Scripture teach us about the use of our freedom in Christ?
   a. Galatians 5:13
   b. 1 Peter 2:15–16

DISCUSSION QUESTIONS

1. Outline Jonathan Edwards' explanation of the way in which the mind and the will work together in the act of making a choice.
2. In what way do desires and inclinations affect the will? Why did Edwards say that we always choose according to our strongest desire at any given moment?
3. Edwards argued that an indifferent choice is an irrational concept. Is this true? Why or why not?

APPLICATION

1. Do you believe that you always choose according to your strongest inclination at the moment? When you choose to sin, is it because at that moment you desire to sin more than you desire to please Christ? How can an understanding of Edwards' teaching help you to overcome temptations to rationalize sinful choices?
2. If your choices are caused by your inclinations and desires, what can you do to strengthen your desires for Christ?
3. Why is it important that you as a believer do not abuse the freedom you have in Christ?

FOR FURTHER STUDY

Sproul, R.C. *Willing to Believe*, pp. 147–165
Edwards, Jonathan. *On the Freedom of the Will*

12

The Pelagian Captivity of the Church

MESSAGE INTRODUCTION

One of the primary reasons for the resurgence of Pelagianism in the modern church is the hugely influential ministry of Charles Finney in the nineteenth century. Many consider him to be America's greatest revivalist, yet few are aware that he adamantly rejected such doctrines as the substitutionary atonement of Christ and justification by faith alone. In this lesson, Dr. Sproul examines the theology of Finney and explains why his influence on American Christianity is extremely dangerous.

LEARNING OBJECTIVES

1. To understand Charles Finney's influence on modern American evangelicalism.
2. To be able to explain Finney's concepts of the Fall, justification, and the Atonement.
3. To be able to outline a Biblical response to Finney's doctrine.

QUOTATIONS

It is, therefore, naturally impossible, and a most palpable contradiction, to affirm that the justification of a sinner, or of one who has violated the law, is a forensic or judicial justification. . . .

—Charles G. Finney

Some theologians have made justification a condition of sanctification, instead of making sanctification a condition of justification, but this . . . is an erroneous view of the subject. . . . That present, full, and entire consecration of heart and life to God and His service, is an unalterable condition of present pardon of past sin, and of present acceptance with God.

—Charles G. Finney

LECTURE OUTLINE

I. Introduction

   A. Among the main contributing factors to the unprecedented degree of Pelagian influence in the modern evangelical church are the ministry, work, and theology of Charles Finney.
   B. Finney has been called America's greatest revivalist, and his methodology of evangelism became the model for all subsequent mass evangelism.
   C. In the nineteenth century, he received sharp criticism from theologians such as B.B. Warfield, who said that God could be entirely eliminated from Finney's theology without substantially changing it.

II. An evangelical hero?

   A. Many American Christians consider Finney to be an evangelical hero, but it is inaccurate even to refer to him as an evangelical.
   B. There are at least three points at which his theology is in direct contradiction with evangelical theology.
      i. Finney espoused pure Pelagianism.
      ii. Finney strongly denied the doctrine of the substitutionary atonement of Christ.
      iii. Finney adamantly rejected the doctrine of justification by faith alone.
   C. Finney is especially strong in his criticisms of *sola fide* and forensic justification, arguing that sinners are not justified, but that they are pardoned.
   D. If *sola fide* is an essential article of historic evangelicalism and Finney rejects it, how can he be considered an evangelical?
   E. Even more importantly, if *sola fide* is the Gospel and Finney rejects it, how can he be considered a Christian?

III. Justification and the Atonement

   A. Finney categorically rejected the "substitutionary satisfaction" view of the Atonement.
   B. He claimed that it would be morally repugnant for our guilt to be imputed to Christ or for Christ's righteousness to be imputed to us.
   C. He advocated a "moral influence" view of the Atonement: the death of Christ demonstrates that God takes sin seriously, he said.
   D. Finney called people to stop sinning and start obeying because God will declare a person just only if he is first sanctified.
   E. In Finney's theology, justification is based on sanctification.

IV. The Fall and original sin

   A. Finney categorically rejected the doctrine of original sin.
   B. He taught that there is nothing inherently corrupt in human nature after the Fall.
   C. According to Finney, man has both the natural ability and the moral ability to be righteous.

D. Finney defined *regeneration* as a change brought about by the choice of a human being to change his ways.
E. In Finney's view, there is no need for the Holy Spirit to change the human nature, because human nature is alive and well.
F. Finney's view is also that of the majority of churches claiming to be evangelical.
G. The problem is that Finney's doctrine involves the intrusion of a pagan view of the will that denies both the impact of the Fall upon man and the subsequent bondage of his will—facts to which the New Testament repeatedly points.

STUDY QUESTIONS

1. Charles Finney has been called America's greatest ____________ by many evangelicals.
    a. Revivalist
    b. Theologian
    c. Philosopher
    d. Pastor

2. Who said that God could be entirely eliminated from Finney's theology without substantially changing it?
    a. Lewis Sperry Chafer
    b. Finney himself
    c. B.B. Warfield
    d. Jonathan Edwards

3. Finney espoused ____________.
    a. Pure Pelagianism
    b. Semi-Pelagianism
    c. Arminianism
    d. Calvinism

4. Finney strongly denied the doctrine of the ____________ of Christ.
    a. Resurrection
    b. Ascension
    c. Deity
    d. Substitutionary atonement

5. Finney argued that sinners are not justified, but that they are ____________.
    a. Glorified
    b. Raised from spiritual death to life
    c. Forensically justified
    d. Pardoned

6. Finney advocated a ____________ view of the Atonement.
   a. Substitutionary
   b. Moral influence
   c. Ransom
   d. Governmental

7. In Finney's theology, justification is based on ____________.
   a. Regeneration
   b. Faith
   c. The imputed righteousness of Christ
   d. Sanctification

8. Whose view is also that of the majority of churches claiming to be evangelical?
   a. Charles Finney's
   b. B.B. Warfield's
   c. Martin Luther's
   d. Augustine's

BIBLE STUDY

1. Read Romans 5:12, 17, and 19. What do these texts of Scripture teach us about the effects of Adam's sin on his descendants?

2. What do the following Scripture passages tell us about the nature of Christ's atoning work? Do these texts indicate a substitutionary view of the atonement?
   a. John 11:50
   b. 2 Corinthians 5:20–21
   c. Galatians 3:13
   d. 1 Peter 3:18

3. How do the following passages of Scripture shed light on the doctrine of the substitutionary Atonement?
   a. Isaiah 53:6, 12
   b. Mark 15:28

4. Read the following texts of Scripture. What do they teach about the nature of justification?
   a. Habakkuk 2:4
   b. Romans 3:22, 28, 30
   c. Romans 4:1–4
   d. Galatians 3:6, 24

DISCUSSION QUESTIONS

1. Charles Finney was one of the most influential figures in American church history. In what ways do you see his influence manifested in the modern evangelical church? Have his views been influential in your local church background?
2. Many Christians who admire Finney are unaware of the statements he made about the doctrine of justification by faith alone and about the atoning work of Christ. Do you believe that his views on these subjects should affect the evangelical church's opinion of Finney? Why or why not?
3. Explain the central teaching of Finney as it relates to the freedom of the will. What are the problems with this understanding of the issues?

APPLICATION

1. Has Charles Finney been an influence on you at any point in your Christian life? Were you aware of his doctrinal views? Does a knowledge of his theology affect your personal estimation of his influence?
2. Would you change anything about the way you present the Gospel based on what you have learned in this lesson?
3. In what ways has this series affected your views? Have your views been challenged? Reinforced? In what way?

FOR FURTHER STUDY

Hodge, A.A. *The Atonement*
Kistler, Don, ed. *Justification by Faith Alone*
Sproul, R.C. *Willing to Believe*, pp. 169–185